MW01224641

JUSTIFICATION
VINDICATED

Robert Traill

THE BANNER OF TRUTH TRUST

THE BANNER OF TRUTH TRUST
3 Murrayfield Road, Edinburgh EH12 6EL
P.O. Box 621, Carlisle, Pennsylvania 17013, USA

*

First published 1692
New revised edition 2002

*

ISBN 0 85151 818 4

*

Typeset in 11/13 pt New Baskerville at
the Banner of Truth Trust, Edinburgh
Printed and bound in Great Britain
by MPG Books Ltd.,
Bodmin, Cornwall

JUSTIFICATION
VINDICATED

Contents

Introduction

Robert Traill (1642–1716), a Scottish Presbyterian pastor and theologian was one of six children, and the middle son, born to Robert Traill and Jean Annan. The elder Traill, himself a Presbyterian pastor, served as a chaplain with the Scottish army during the English Civil War and as minister of Greyfriars Church, Edinburgh. At the Restoration Charles II first imprisoned, and then banished, Traill for reminding him publicly of his sworn obligations under the Solemn League and Covenant.

His son Robert, the author of this work, lived during the so-called Killing Times in Scotland. A younger friend of William Guthrie (1620–65), author of *The Christian's Great Interest*,[1] Traill witnessed the public execution of Guthrie's cousin, James Guthrie, in 1661. Then, a suspected confederate in the Covenanters' Pentland Rising, he fled to Holland following a charge of treason. There Traill studied theology at the University of Utrecht and assisted in the republication of Samuel Rutherford's *Examination of Arminianism* (1668).

[1] 1658; republished by the Banner of Truth Trust in the Puritan Paperback series (ISBN 0 85151 354 9, 208 pp.).

In 1670, following Presbyterian ordination in London, he accepted a call to pastor a church in Cranbrook, Kent. Visiting Edinburgh in 1677, Traill was arrested for preaching in a private home and imprisoned for several months on the Bass Rock. After his release, he returned to London to assist Nathaniel Mather at an Independent congregation and then following Mather's death, to gather a separate Scottish congregation.

The republication in 1690 of the works of Tobias Crisp (1600–43) undermined a proposed plan of merger between Presbyterian and Independent churches in England by sparking a conflict known as the *Neonomian Controversy*. It was in this historical context that Robert Traill's masterful *Vindication of the Protestant Doctrine concerning Justification from the Unjust Charge of Antinomianism* (1692)[1], now republished in the present form, defended the Reformed doctrine of justification by faith on two fronts.

Traill's treatise guarded the doctrine of justification by faith, on the one hand, from misappropriation by antinomians like Tobias Crisp. Dr Crisp reportedly made such a muddle of the believer's union with Christ that he was said to have 'made a Saviour of the sinner, and a sinner of the Saviour. He speaks as if God considered the sinner as doing and suffering what Christ did and suffered; and Christ as having committed their sins, and as actually being guilty of them' (Benjamin Brooks, *Lives of the Puritans*, Volume 2, page 475).

---

[1] Written originally as 'a letter from the author to a minister in the country'; see p. 1.

Traill's work defended the doctrine of justification by faith, on the other hand, against a danger no less threatening, that of the legalism (or Arminianism) of men like Richard Baxter. These viewed faith, in the guise of new gospel obedience, as the ground of justification rather than Christ's imputed righteousness. In fact, they looked askance at the imputed righteousness of Christ, much as John Wesley did half a century later, as though it were an open invitation to licentiousness.

As the magisterial Protestant Reformers Luther and Calvin understood so well, the Christian church stands or falls with the doctrine of justification by faith. We live in perilous postmodern times. Ecumenicity and pluralism prevail to the extent that historic differences over Scripture and doctrinal confessions are papered over rather than honestly faced and defended. In the recent Lutheran-Roman Catholic dialogue, for example, Luther's *Ninety-Five Theses* were transmogrified by strange ecclesiastical priestcraft into 'Ninety-Five Reasons Why We Ought To Love One Another'.

John Owen, the great Puritan theologian, expressed his own scepticism even about more serious theological attempts (one thinks immediately of *Evangelicals and Catholics Together*) to resolve the rift between Protestant and Roman Catholic understandings of justification. He regarded Protestant concessions as fruitless, so long as the Tridentine canons and decrees remained in full force and effect:

> [Despite concessions on both sides] the distance and breach continue as wide as ever they were. Nor is there the least ground toward peace obtained by any of our

[concessions]. For unless we can come up entirely unto the decrees of the Council of Trent, wherein the doctrine of the Old and New Testament is anathematized, they will make no other use of any man's [concessions], but only to increase the clamour of differences among ourselves. I mention [this] . . . only to intimate the uselessness of such concessions in order unto peace and agreement with them, whilst they have a Procrustes' bed to lay us upon, and from whose size they will not recede.[1]

There is an urgent need for the Reformed churches to champion again the doctrine of justification by faith. Jesus' prophetic doom against the scribes and Pharisees was pronounced precisely because they, like the Church of Rome today, corrupted the doctrine of justification by faith: 'But woe to you, scribes and Pharisees, hypocrites, because you shut up the kingdom of heaven against men; for you neither go in yourselves, nor do you allow those who are entering to go in' (*Matt.* 23:13).

Traill himself deemed the doctrine of justification vitally important. He fully considered it to be the very crux of the Christian gospel:

All the great fundamentals of Christian truth centre in this of justification. The Trinity of persons in the Godhead; the incarnation of the only begotten of the Father; the satisfaction paid to the law and justice of God, for the sins of the world, by his obedience and sacrifice of himself in that flesh he assumed; and the

[1] Owen, *Works* (reprinted London: Banner of Truth, 1965), vol. 5, pp. 68.

divine authority of the Scriptures which reveal all this: these are all straight lines of truth that centre in this doctrine of justification of a sinner by the imputation and application of that satisfaction. There can be no justification without a righteousness; no righteousness can suffice but that which answers fully and perfectly the holy law of God; no such righteousness can be performed, but by a divine person; no benefit can accrue to a sinner by it unless it is in some way his, and applied to him; no application can be made of this but by faith in Jesus Christ.

But this is not all. Not only must we uphold justification through the imputation of Christ's righteousness as necessary to defend the gospel. The denial of this crucial biblical doctrine has serious – and deadly – practical consequences. Traill continues:

And as the connection with and dependence of this truth upon the other great mysteries of divine truth is evident . . . so the forsaking of the doctrine of justification by faith in Christ's righteousness has been the first step of apostasy in many . . . Hence so many Arminians . . . turned Socinians. From denying justification by Christ's righteousness, they proceeded to the denying of his satisfaction; from the denial of his proper satisfaction, they went on to the denying of the divinity of his person.

In their slide into Socinianism (or Unitarianism) the Arminians had plenty of company. Tragically, many

English Presbyterians, influenced by Baxter's Neo-nomianism, joined ranks with them. All of which should humble into the dust those of us who hold the precious truths of the Reformation dear and bestir us to seek, in defending the faith once delivered to the saints, the Lord's upholding grace: 'Let him who thinks he stands take heed lest he fall' (*1 Cor.* 10:12).

It is hoped that a renewed acquaintance with Traill's treatise will invigorate the Reformed churches to uphold the doctrine of justification by the imputed righteousness of Christ and, by extension, the glory of the only Mediator between God and man, our Lord and Saviour Jesus Christ.

THE PUBLISHER
February 2002

I

The Rise of the Controversy

Your earnest desire of information about some difference amongst Nonconformists in London, whereof you hear so much by flying reports, and profess you know so little of the truth thereof, is the cause of this writing.[1]

You know that not many months ago there was a fair appearance of unity between the two most considerable parties on that side; and their differences, having been rather in practice than principle, about church-order and communion, seemed easily reconcilable, where a spirit of love, and of a sound mind, was at work. But how short was the calm! For quickly there arose a greater storm from another quarter; and a quarrel began upon higher points, even on no less than the doctrine of the grace of God in Jesus Christ, and the

[1] The *Neonomian Controversy* (see *Introduction*, pp. viii, ix).

justification of a sinner by faith alone. Some think that the reprinting of Dr Crisp's[1] book gave the first rise to it. But we must look farther back for its true spring. It is well known, but little considered, what a great progress Arminianism had made in this nation before the beginning of the civil war. And surely it has lost little since it ended. What can be the reason why the very parliaments in the reigns of James I and Charles I were so alarmed with Arminianism, as may be read in history, and is remembered by old men; and that now for a long time there has been no talk, no fear of it; as if Arminianism were dead and buried, and no man knows where its grave is? Is not the true reason to be found in its universal prevailing in the nation?

But that which concerns our case is that the middle way between the Arminians and the Orthodox had been espoused, and strenuously defended and promoted, by some Nonconformists, of great note for piety and parts; and usually such men that are for middle ways in points of doctrine have a greater kindness for that extreme they go halfway to, than for that which they go halfway from. And the notions thereof were imbibed by a great many students, who laboured (through the iniquity of the times) under the great disadvantage of the want of grave and sound divines to direct and assist their studies at universities; and therefore contented themselves with studying such English authors as had gone in a path untrod, both by our predecessors, and by the Protestant universities abroad.

[1] Tobias Crisp (1600–43), an Antinomian writer who earlier in his ministry had been an Arminian.

These notions have been preached, and written against by several divines amongst themselves; and the different opinions have been, till of late, managed with some moderation; to which our being all borne down by persecution did somewhat contribute.

It is a sad but true observation that no contentions are more easily kindled, more fiercely pursued, and more hardly composed, than those of divines; sometimes from their zeal for truth; and sometimes from worse principles that may act in them as well as in other men.

2

Justification by Faith Alone Not Lawlessness

The subject of the controversy is the justifying grace of God in Jesus Christ. Owned it is by both sides; and both fear it is abused, either by turning it into wantonness, hence the noise of Antinomianism, or by corrupting it with the mixture of works, hence the fears, on the other side, of Arminianism. Both parties disown the name cast upon them. The one will not be called Arminian, and the other hate both name and thing of Antinomianism, truly so called. Both sometimes say the same thing, and profess their assent to the doctrinal articles of the Church of England, to the Confession of Faith and Catechisms composed at Westminster, and to the harmony of the Confessions of all the Reformed churches in these doctrines of grace. And if both are candid in this profession it is very strange that there should be any controversy amongst them.

THE PARTIES

Let us therefore, first, take a view of the parties, and then of their principles. As to the party suspected of Antinomianism and Libertinism in this city, it is plain that the churches wherein they are concerned are more strict and exact in examining those that offer themselves unto their communion, as to their faith and holiness, before their admitting them; in the engagements laid on them to a gospel-walking at their admission; and in their inspection over them afterwards. As to their conversation, they are generally of the more regular and exact frame; and the fruits of holiness in their lives, to the praise of God and honour of the gospel, cannot with modesty be denied.[1]

Is it not unaccountable to charge a people with licentiousness, when the chargers cannot deny, and some cannot well bear, the strictness of their walk? It is commonly said, that it is only their principles and the tendency of them to loose walking that they blame. But, waiving that at present, it seems unfair to charge a people with licentious doctrines when the professors thereof are approved of for their godliness; and when they sincerely profess that their godliness began with and is promoted by the faith of their principles. Let it not be mistaken if I here make a comparison between Papists and Protestants.

The latter did always profess the doctrine of justification by faith alone. This was blasphemy in the Papists'

---

[1] Though a Presbyterian, Traill sided in this dispute with the Independent churches and here defends them from the false charge of Antinomianism. These churches should not be regarded as following the teachings of Tobias Crisp. See Traill's balanced assessment, p. 18.

ears. They did, and still do, cry out against it as a licentious doctrine and destructive of good works. Many sufficient answers have been given to this unjust charge. But to my purpose: The wonder was that the Papists were not convinced by the splendid holiness of the old believers, and by the visible truth of their holy practice; and their professing that as long as they lived in the blindness and darkness of popery they were profane; and that as soon as God revealed the gospel to them, and had wrought in them the faith thereof, they were sanctified, and led other lives.

So witnessed the noble Lord Cobham who suffered in King Henry V's time, more than a hundred years before Luther. His words at his examination before the Archbishop of Canterbury and his clergy were these: 'As for that virtuous man Wycliffe [for with his doctrine he was charged], whose judgment ye so highly disdain; I shall say of my part, both before God and man, that before I knew that despised doctrine of his, I never abstained from sin; but since I learned therein to fear my Lord God, it hath otherwise, I trust, been with me. So much grace could I never find in all your glorious instructions' (Foxe's *Book of Martyrs*, vol. 1, p. 640, col. 2, 1664 edition). And since I am on that excellent book, I entreat you to read Mr Patrick Hamilton's little treatise,[1] to which Frith[2] wrote a preface and Foxe added some explication (vol. 2, p. 181–192); where you will find the old, plain, Protestant truth about law and gospel,

[1] Patrick Hamilton (d. 1528), the first martyr of the Scottish Reformation, whose book *Diverse Fruitful Gatherings of Scripture* was published soon after his death.

[2] John Frith (d. 1533), an early English Protestant martyr.

delivered without any school-terms. To this, add, in your reading, in the same vol. 2, p. 497–509: *Heresies and errors falsely charged on Tyndale's writings*, where we will see the old faith of the saints in its simplicity and the old craft and cunning of the Anti-Christian party, in slandering the truth. I must, for my part, confess, that these plain declarations of gospel truth have a quite other favour with me than the dry, insipid accounts thereof given by pretenders to human wisdom.

GUIDING PRINCIPLES

But passing these things, let us look to principles, and that with respect to their native and regular influence on sanctification. And I am willing that that should determine the matter, next to the consonancy of the principles themselves with the Word of God. It can be no doctrine of God that is not according to godliness. Some think that if good works, and holiness, and repentance, be allowed no room in justification, then there is no room left for them in the world, and in the practice of believers, so hard it seems to be to some to keep in their eye the certain fixed boundaries between justification and sanctification. There is no difference between a justified and a sanctified man, for he is always the same person that partakes of these privileges. But justification and sanctification differ greatly, in many respects, as is commonly known. But to come a little closer:

The party here suspected of Antinomianism do confidently protest, before God, angels and men, that they espouse no new doctrine about the grace of God and justification and the other coincident points, but what the Reformers at home and abroad did teach, and all the Protestant churches do own. And that in sum is:

> That a law-condemned sinner is freely justified by God's grace, through the redemption that is in Jesus Christ;
> That he is justified only for the righteousness of Christ imputed to him by God of his free grace, and received by faith alone as an instrument, which faith is the gift of the same grace.

To guard against licentiousness they constantly teach, out of God's Word:

> That without holiness no man can see God;
> That all that believe truly on Jesus Christ, as they are justified by the sprinkling of his blood, so are they sanctified by the effusion of his Spirit;
> That all that boast of their faith in Christ, and yet live after their own lusts and the course of this world, have no true faith at all, but do, in their profession, and practice, blaspheme the name of God, and the doctrine of his grace; and, continuing so, shall perish with a double destruction, beyond that of the openly profane that make no profession.

And when they find any such in their communion, which is exceeding rarely, they cast them out as dead branches. They teach:

> That as the daily study of sanctification is a necessary exercise to all that are in Christ; so the rule of their direction therein is the holy, spotless law of God in Christ's hand;

9

That the Holy Ghost is the beginner and advancer of this work, and faith in Jesus Christ the great means thereof;

That no man can be holy till he be in Christ, and united to him by faith;

And that no man is truly in Christ, but he is thereby sanctified.

They preach the law, to condemn all flesh out of Christ, and to show thereby to people the necessity of betaking themselves to him for salvation. See the savoury words of blessed Tyndale, called the apostle of England, in his letter to John Frith, written in January 1533 (*Book of Martyrs*, vol. 2, p. 808):

Expound the law truly, and open the veil of Moses, to condemn all flesh, and prove all men sinners, and all deeds under the law, before mercy have taken away the condemnation thereof, to be sin and damnable; and then as a faithful minister, set abroach[1] the mercy of our Lord Jesus, and let the wounded consciences drink of the water of him. And then shall your preaching be with power, and not as the hypocrites. And the Spirit of God shall work with you; and all consciences shall bear record unto you, and feel that it is so. And all doctrine that casteth a mist on these two, to shadow and hide them, I mean the law of God, and mercy of Christ; that resist you with all your power.

And so we do.

---

[1] To set abroach = to pierce (a cask, etc.), so as to let the contents flow out.

3

Real Differences on Justification

What is there in all this to be offended with? Is not this enough to vindicate our doctrine from any tendency to licentiousness? I am afraid that there are some things wherein we differ more than they think fit yet to express. And I shall guess at them.

1. The first is about *the imputed righteousness of Christ.*

This righteousness of Christ, in his active and passive obedience, has been asserted by Protestant divines to be not only the procuring and meritorious *cause* of our justification (for this the Papists admit) but the *matter,* as the imputation of it is the *form,* of our justification; though I think that our logical terms are not so adapted for such divine mysteries. But whatever propriety or impropriety there is in such school-terms, the common Protestant doctrine has been that a convinced sinner, seeking justification, must have nothing in his eye but this righteousness of Christ, as God proposes nothing else to him, and that God in justifying a sinner accepts him in this righteousness alone, when he imputes it to him.

Now, about the imputed righteousness of Christ, some say[1] that it belongs only to the person of Christ. He was under the law and bound to keep it for himself, so that he might be a fit Mediator, without spot or blemish; that it is a qualification in the Mediator, rather than a benefit acquired by him, to be communicated to his people. For they will not allow this personal righteousness of Christ to be imputed to us any otherwise than in the merit of it, as purchasing for us a more easy law of grace, in the observation of which they place all our justifying righteousness, understanding hereby our own personal inherent holiness and nothing else.

They hold that Christ died to merit this of the Father, namely, that we might be justified upon easier terms under the gospel than those of the law of innocency. Instead of justification by perfect obedience, we are now to be justified by our own evangelical righteousness, made up of faith, repentance, and sincere obedience. And if we hold not with them in this, they tell the world that we are enemies to evangelical holiness, slighting the practice of all good works, and allowing our hearers to live as they please.

[1] What follows is a summary and critique of the views of Richard Baxter.

Thus they slander the preachers of free grace, because we do not place justification in our own inherent holiness; but in Christ's perfect righteousness, imputed to us upon our believing in him. This faith, we teach, purifies the heart, and always inclines to holiness of life. Neither do we hold any faith to be true and saving, that does not show itself by good works; without which no man is or can be justified, either in his own conscience or before men.

But it does not follow from this that we cannot be justified in the sight of God by faith only, since the apostle Paul asserts the latter, and the apostle James the former, in a good agreement.

2. There appears to be some difference, or misunderstanding of one another, about *the true notion and nature of justifying faith.*

Divines commonly distinguish between the *direct* act of faith and the *reflex* act. The direct act is properly justifying and saving faith, by which a lost sinner comes to Christ and relies upon him for salvation. The reflex act is the looking back of the soul upon a former act of faith. A rational creature can reflect upon his own acts, whether they are acts of reason, faith, or unbelief. A direct act of saving faith is that by which a lost sinner goes out of himself to Christ for help, relying upon him only for salvation. A reflex act arises from the sense that faith gives of its own inward act, upon a serious review. The truth and sincerity of this is further cleared up to the conscience by the genuine fruits of an unfeigned faith, appearing to all men in our good lives, and holy conversation. But, as plain as these things are, yet we find we are frequently mistaken by others, and we wonder at the mistake; for we dare not ascribe to some learned and good men the principles of ignorance or wilfulness, from which mistakes in plain cases usually proceed. When we press sinners to come to Christ by a direct act of faith, consisting in a humble reliance upon him for mercy and pardon, they will understand us, whether we will or not, of a reflex act of faith, by which a man knows and believes that his sins are pardoned, and that Christ is his, when they might easily know that we mean no such thing. Mr Walter Marshall, in his excellent book, *The Gospel Mystery of Sanctification*,[1] lately published, has largely opened this, and the true controversy of this day, though it be eight or nine years since he died.

3. We seem to differ about *the interest, and room, and place, that faith has in justification.*

That we are justified by faith in Jesus Christ is so plainly a New Testament truth that no man pretending however barely to the Christian name denies it. The Papists own it; and the Socinians, and Arminians, and all own it. But how different are their senses of it! And indeed you cannot more speedily and certainly judge of the spirit of a man than by his real inward sense of this phrase (if you could reach it), 'A sinner is justified by faith in Jesus Christ.'

Some say that faith in Jesus Christ justifies as it is a work, by the act of believing; as if it came in the place of

[1]Reprinted Welwyn: Evangelical Press, 1981.

perfect obedience, required by the law. Some say that faith justifies as it is informed and animated by charity. This is the teaching of the Papists, who plainly confound justification and sanctification. Some say, that faith justifies as it is a fulfilling of the condition of the new covenant: If you believe you shall be saved. Nay, they will not stop there, but they will have this faith to justify as it has a principle and fitness in it to dispose to sincere obedience.

The plain old Protestant doctrine is that the place of faith in justification is only that of a hand or instrument, receiving the righteousness of Christ, for the sake of which alone we are justified. So that, though great scholars do often confound themselves and others in their disputations about faith's justifying a sinner, every poor plain believer has the marrow of this mystery feeding his heart; and he can readily tell you that to be justified by faith is to be justified by Christ's righteousness, apprehended by faith.

4. We seem to misunderstand one another about *the two Adams, and especially the latter.*

See Romans 5, verse 12 to the end. In that excellent scripture a comparison is instituted which, if we did duly understand and agree in it, we should not readily differ in the main things of the gospel. The apostle there tells us that the first Adam stood in the place of all his natural posterity. He had their stock in his hand. While he stood they stood in him; when he fell, they fell with him. By his fall he derived sin and death to all those that spring from him by natural generation. This is the sad side. But he tells us, in opposition to that, and by way of comparison with it, that Christ, the second man, is the new head of the redeemed world. He stands in their place. His obedience is theirs; and he communicates to his spiritual offspring the very contrary to that which the first sinful Adam does to his natural offspring: righteousness instead of guilt and sin, life instead of death, justification instead of condemnation, and eternal life instead of hell deserved.

So that I think the third, fourth and fifth chapters of the epistle to the Romans, for the mystery of justification; and the sixth, seventh and eighth, for the mystery of sanctification, deserve our deep study.

But what say others about Christ's being the second Adam? We find them unwilling to speak of it; and when they do, it is quite alien from the scope of the apostle in that chapter. Thus to us they seem to say:

> That God as a rector, ruler, governor, has resolved to save men by Jesus Christ;
> That the rule of this government is the gospel, as a new law of grace;
> That Jesus Christ is set as the head of this rectoral government;
> That in that state he sits in glory, ready and able, out of his purchase and merits, to give justification and eternal life to all that can bring good evidence of their having complied with the terms and conditions of the law of grace.

Thus they anticipate the last day, and hold forth Christ as a Judge rather than a Saviour. Luther was wont to warn people of this distinction frequently in his commentary on the epistle to the Galatians. And no other headship of Christ do we find some willing to admit than what belongs to his kingly office. As for his suretyship, and being the second Adam, and a public person, some treat it with contempt.

I have heard that Dr Thomas Goodwin was in his youth an Arminian, or at least inclining that way, but was by the Lord's grace brought off by Dr Sibbes' clearing up to him this same point of Christ's being the head and representative of all his people. Now, though we maintain steadfastly this headship of Jesus Christ, yet we do not say that there is an actual partaking of his fulness of grace till we are in him by faith; though this faith is also given us on Christ's behalf (*Phil.* 1:29), and we believe through grace (*Acts* 18:27). And we know no grace, we can call nothing grace, we care for no grace, but what comes from this head, the Saviour of the body. But so much shall serve to point out the main things of difference and mistakes.

Is it not a little provoking that some are so captious that no minister can preach in the hearing of some of the freedom of God's grace, of the imputation of Christ's righteousness, of sole and single believing on him for righteousness and eternal life, of the impossibility of a natural man's doing any good work before he is in Christ, of the impossibility of the mixing of man's righteousness and works with Christ's righteousness in the business of justification, and several other points, but he is immediately called, or suspected to be, an

Antinomian? If we say that faith in Jesus Christ is neither work, nor condition, nor qualification, in justification; but is a mere instrument, receiving (as an empty hand receives the freely given alms) the righteousness of Christ; and that, in its very act, it is a renouncing of all things but the gift of grace; the fire is kindled. So that it is come to this, as Mr Christopher Fowler said, that he that will not be Antichristian must be called an Antinomian.

Is there a minister in London, who did not preach, some twenty, some thirty years ago, according to their standing, that same doctrine now by some called Antinomian? Let not Dr Crisp's book be looked upon as the standard of our doctrine. There are many good things in it, and also many expressions in it that we generally dislike. It is true that Mr Burgess[1] and Mr Rutherford[2] wrote against Antinomianism, and against some that were both Antinomians and Arminians.

And it is no less true that they wrote against the Arminians, and did hate the new scheme of divinity so much now contended for, and to which we owe all our present contentions. I am persuaded that if these godly and sound divines were on the present stage, they would be as ready to draw their pens against two books lately printed against Dr Crisp as ever they were to write

[1] Anthony Burgess, Puritan minister, member of the Westminster Assembly and author of *Vindiciae Legis, A Vindication of the Moral Law* (1646).

[2] Samuel Rutherford, Scottish Presbyterian minister, Commissioner to the Westminster Assembly and Professor of Divinity, author of *A Display of Spiritual Antichrist* (1648) and *An Examination of Arminianism* (1668).

against the Doctor's book. Truth is to be defended by truth; but error is often, and unhappily, opposed by error under truth's name.

But what shall we do in this case? What shall we do for peace with our brethren? Shall we lie still under their undeserved reproaches; and, for keeping the peace, silently suffer others to beat us unjustly? If it were our own personal concern, we should bear it. If it were only their charging us with ignorance, weakness, and being unstudied divines (as they have used liberally to call all that have not learned, and dare not believe, their new divinity), we might easily pass it by, or put up with it. But when we see the pure gospel of Christ corrupted and an Arminian gospel newly patched up and obtruded on people, to the certain peril of the souls of such as believe it; and our ministry reflected upon, which should be dearer to us than our lives, can we be silent?

As we have a charge from the Lord to deliver to our people what we have received from him, so, as he calls and enables, we are not to give place by subjection, even for an hour, to such as creep in, not only to spy out, but to destroy, not so much the gospel *liberty* as the gospel *salvation* we have in Christ Jesus, and to bring us back under the yoke of legal bondage (*Gal.* 2:4–5). And indeed the case in that epistle to the Galatians and ours have a great affinity.

Is it desired that we should forbear to make a free offer of God's grace in Christ to the worst of sinners? This cannot be granted by us: for this is the gospel faithful saying, and worthy of all acceptation (and therefore worthy of all our preaching of it), that Jesus Christ came into the world to save sinners and the chief of them (*1 Tim.* 1:15). This was the apostolic practice, according to their Lord's command (*Mark* 16:15–16; *Luke* 24:47). They began at Jerusalem, where the Lord of life was wickedly slain by them; and yet life in and through his blood was offered to, and accepted and obtained by, many of them. Every believer's experience witnesses to this, that every one that believes on Jesus Christ acts that faith as the chief of sinners. Every man that sees himself rightly thinks so of himself, and therein does not think amiss. God only knows who is truly the greatest sinner, and every humbled sinner will think that he is the man.

Shall we tell men that unless they are holy they must not believe on Jesus Christ? That they must not venture on Christ for salvation till they are qualified and fit to be received and welcomed by him? This would be to forbear preaching the gospel at all, or to forbid all men to believe on Christ. For never was any sinner qualified for Christ. *He* is well qualified for *us* (*1 Cor.* 1:30); but a sinner out of Christ has no qualification for Christ but sin and misery. Whence should we have any better, but in and from Christ? Nay, suppose an impossibility, that a man were qualified for Christ; I boldly assert, that such a man would not, nor could ever, believe on Christ. For faith is a lost, helpless condemned sinner's casting himself on Christ for salvation; and the qualified man is not such a person.

Shall we warn people, that they should not believe on Christ too soon? It is impossible that they should do it too soon. Can a man obey the great gospel command too soon (*1 John* 3: 23)? Or do the great work of God too soon (*John* 6:28–29)? A man may too soon think that he is in Christ; and that is when it is not so indeed; and this we frequently teach. But this is but an idle dream, and not faith. A man may too soon fancy that he has faith; but, I hope, he cannot act faith too soon. If any should say a man may be holy too soon, how would that saying be reflected upon? And yet it is certain that, though no man can be too soon holy (because he cannot too soon believe on Christ, which is the only spring of true holiness), yet he may, and many do, set about the study of that which he counts holiness too soon; that is, before the tree is changed (*Matt.* 12:33–35); before he has the new heart (*Ezek.* 36:26–27), and the Spirit of God dwelling in him, which is only obtained by faith in Christ (*Gal.* 3:14); and therefore all this man's studying of holiness is not only vain labour but acting of sin.

And if this study, and these endeavours, be managed as commonly they are, to obtain justification before God, they are the more wicked works still. And because this point is needful to be known, I would give you some testimonies for it. First, the doctrine of the Church of England in her *Thirty-Nine Articles*, Article 13:

> Works done before the grace of Christ, and the inspiration of his Spirit, are not pleasant to God; forasmuch as they spring not of faith in Jesus Christ: neither do they make men meet to receive grace, or (as the school-authors say) deserve grace of congruity. Yea, rather, for that they are not done as God hath willed and commanded them to be done, we doubt not but they have the nature of sin.

So also the *Westminster Confession of Faith*, xvi:7.

And Calvin (*Institutes*, III.xv.6), speaking of the Popish schoolmen, says:

> They have found out I know not what moral good works, whereby men are made acceptable to God before they are ingrafted into Christ. As if the Scripture lied when it said, They are all in death who have not the Son, 1 John 5:12. If they be in death, how can they beget matter of life? As if it were of no force, Whatsoever is not of faith is sin; as if evil trees could bring forth good fruit.

Read the rest of that section. To the contrary, the Council of Trent, Session 6, Canon 7, says boldly, 'Whosoever shall say, That all works done before justification, howsoever they be done, are truly sin, and deserve the hatred of God, let him be anathema.' And to give you one more bellowing of the beast, wounded by the light of the gospel, see the same council, Session 6, Canon 11: *Si quis dixerit, Gratiam qua justificamur esse tantum favorem Dei; anathema sit* (Whosoever shall say, That the grace by which we are justified is the mere favour of God, let him be anathema).

'This is fearful blasphemy', says Dr Downham[1], Bishop of Londonderry, in his orthodox book on justification, 3:1, where he says, 'The Hebrew words which in the Old Testament signify the grace of God do always signify favour, and never grace inherent. And above fifty testimonies may be brought from the New Testament to prove that by God's *grace* his *favour* is still meant.' But what was good Church of England doctrine at and after

---

[1] George Downham, author of *The Covenant of Grace*, Dublin, 1631.

the Reformation cannot now go down with some Arminianizing Nonconformists.

If then nothing will satisfy our quarrelling brethren but either silence as to the main points of the gospel, which we believe, and live by the faith of, and look to be saved in; which we have for many years preached with some seals of the Holy Ghost in converting sinners to God, and in building them up in holiness and comfort, by the faith and power of them; which also we vowed to the Lord to preach to all that will hear us, as long as we live, in the day when we gave up ourselves to serve God with our spirit in the gospel of his Son: if either this silence, or the swallowing down of Arminian schemes of the gospel, contrary to the New Testament, and unknown to the Reformed churches, in their greatest purity, be the only terms of peace with our brethren, we must then maintain our peace with God, and our own consciences, in the defence of plain gospel-truth, and our harmony with the Reformed churches; and in the comfort of these bear their enmity.

And though it is usual with them to vilify and contemn such as differ from them, for their fewness, weakness, and want of learning; yet they might know, that the most learned and godly in the Christian world have maintained and defended the same doctrine we stand for, for some ages. The grace of God will never want, for it can, and will furnish, defenders of it. England has been blessed with a Bradwardine,[1] an Archbishop of Canterbury against the Pelagians; a

---

[1] Thomas Bradwardine (c.1290–1349), briefly Archbishop of Canterbury and author of the voluminous *De Causa Dei Contra Pelagium.*

Twisse[1] and Ames[2], against the Arminians. And though they that contend with us would separate their cause altogether from that of these two pests of the church of Christ, I mean Pelagius and Arminius, yet judicious observers cannot but already perceive a coincidency; and do fear more, when either the force of argument shall drive them out of their lurking-holes, or when they shall think fit to discover their secret sentiments, which yet we but guess at.

Then, as we shall know better what they would be at, so it is very likely that they will then find enemies in many whom they have seduced by their craft, and still seem to be in their camp; and will meet with opposers, both at home and abroad, that they think not of.

[1] William Twisse, the first presiding officer (prolocutor) of the Westminster Assembly. Though otherwise a sound divine, Twisse unfortunately asserted that justification is from eternity, that is, *before* faith. In other words, Twisse dispensed with the necessity of the application of redemption in real historical time. The Westminster Confession (xi:iv) corrected this by stating: 'God did, from all eternity, decree to justify the elect . . . nevertheless they are not justified until the Holy Spirit doth in due time actually apply Christ unto them.' (See J. I. Packer, *A Quest for Godliness: The Puritan Vision of the Christian Life*. Wheaton, Ill.: Crossway, 1990, p. 155.)

[2] William Ames (1576–1633), author of *The Marrow of Sacred Theology*, 1623.

4

Advantages of the True Doctrine of Justification

Our doctrine of the justification of a sinner by the free grace of God in Jesus Christ, however it may be misrepresented and reproached, is yet undeniably recommended by four things.

1. *It is a doctrine savoury and precious to all serious, godly persons.*

Dr Ames's observation holds good as to all the Arminian divinity, that it is *contra communem sensum fidelium*, against the common sense of believers. And though this is an argument of little weight with those that value more the judgment of the scribes, and the wise, and the disputers of this world (*1 Cor.* 1:18–21) than of all the godly, yet the Spirit of God by John gives us this same argument (*1 John* 4:5–6): 'They are of the world: therefore speak they of the world, and the world heareth them. We are of God: he that knoweth God, heareth us; he that is not of God heareth not us. Hereby know we the Spirit of truth, and the spirit of error.'

How evident it is that several who, having by education or an unsound ministry had their natural enmity against the grace of God strengthened, when the Lord by his Spirit has broken in upon their hearts and has raised a serious soul-exercise about their salvation, their turning to God in Christ and their turning from Arminianism have begun together. And some of the greatest champions for the grace of God have been persons thus dealt with, of whom we might give examples. And as it is thus with men at their conversion, so it is found afterwards that, while it remains well with them in their inner man, so does the doctrine of grace still appear more precious and savoury. On the other side, all the ungodly and unrenewed have a dislike and disrelish of this doctrine and are all for the doctrine of doing, and love to hear it; and, in their sorry exercise, are still for doing their own business in salvation, though they are nothing, and can do nothing but sin, and destroy themselves.

2. *It is that doctrine only by which a convinced sinner can be dealt with effectually.*

When a man is awakened and brought to that question to which all must be brought, if they are not to come to a worse state, 'What shall I do to be saved?', we have the apostolic answer, 'Believe on the Lord Jesus Christ, and thou shalt be saved, and thy house'

(*Acts* 16:30–31), This answer is so old that with many it seems out of date. But it is still, and will ever be, fresh and new and savoury, and the only resolution of this grand case of conscience, as long as conscience and the world last. No wit or art of man will ever find a crack or flaw in it, or devise another or a better answer, nor can any but this alone rightly heal the wound of an awakened conscience.

Let us set this man to seek resolution in this case from some of the masters in our Israel. According to their principles they must say to him, 'Repent, and mourn for your known sins, and leave them and loathe them; and God will have mercy on you.' 'Alas!' says the poor man, 'my heart is hard, and I cannot repent aright. Yea, I find my heart more hard and vile than when I was secure in sin.' If you speak to this man of qualifications for Christ, he knows nothing of them; if of sincere obedience, his answer is native and ready, 'Obedience is the work of a living man, and sincerity is only in a renewed soul.' Sincere obedience is therefore as impossible to a dead unrenewed sinner as perfect obedience is.

Why should not the right answer be given, 'Believe on the Lord Jesus Christ, and you shall be saved'? Tell him what Christ is, what he has done and suffered to obtain eternal redemption for sinners, and that according to the will of God and his Father. Give him a plain downright narrative of the gospel salvation wrought out by the Son of God; tell him the history and mystery of the gospel plainly. It may be the Holy Ghost will work faith thereby, as he did in those first-fruits of the Gentiles in

Acts 10:44. If he asks what warrant he has to believe on Jesus Christ, tell him that he has an utter indispensable necessity for it, for without believing on him he must perish eternally; that he has God's gracious offer of Christ and all his redemption, with a promise that, upon accepting the offer by faith, Christ and salvation with him are his: that he has God's express commandment (*1 John* 3:23) to believe on Christ's name, and that he should make conscience of obeying it, as much as any command in the moral law. Tell him of Christ's ability and goodwill to save; that no man was ever rejected by him who cast himself upon him; that desperate cases are the glorious triumphs of his art of saving.

Tell him that there is no middle-state between faith and unbelief, that there is no excuse for neglecting the one and continuing in the other, that believing on the Lord Jesus for salvation is more pleasing to God than all obedience to his law, and that unbelief is the most provoking to God and the most damning to man of all sins. Against the greatness of his sins, the curse of the law, and the severity of God as Judge, there is no relief to be held forth to him but the free and boundless grace of God in the merit of Christ's satisfaction by the sacrifice of himself.

If he should say, 'What is it to believe on Jesus Christ?', I find no such question in the Word. All did in some way understand the notion of it: the Jews that did not believe on him (*John* 6:28–30); the chief priests and Pharisees (*John* 7:48); the blind man (*John* 10:35). When Christ asked him, 'Believest thou on the Son of God?', he answered, 'Who is he, Lord, that I may believe on him?' Immediately, when Christ had told him, verse 37, he does not say, 'What is it to believe on him?' but, 'Lord, I believe', and worshipped him. And so he both professed and put into practice faith in him. So the father of the lunatic (*Mark* 9:23–24), and the eunuch (*Acts* 8:37). They all, both Christ's enemies and his disciples, knew that faith in him was a believing that the man Jesus of Nazareth was the Son of God, the Messiah, the Saviour of the world, so as to receive, and look for salvation in his name (*Acts* 4:12). This was the common report, published by Christ and his apostles and disciples, and known by all that heard it.

If he still asks what he is to believe, tell him that he is not called to believe that he is in Christ, that his sins are pardoned, and he a justified man; but that he is to believe God's record concerning Christ (*1 John* 5:10–12), and this record is that God gives (that is, offers) to us eternal life in his Son Jesus Christ, and that all that with the heart believe this report, and rest their souls on these glad tidings, shall be saved (*Rom.* 10:9–11). And thus he is to believe that he may be justified (*Gal.* 2:16).

If he still says that this believing is hard, this is a good doubt, but easily resolved. It bespeaks a man deeply humbled. Anybody may see his own inability to obey the law of God fully, but few find the difficulty of believing. To resolve his doubt, ask him what it is he finds makes believing difficult to him. Is it unwillingness to be justified and saved? Is it unwillingness to be so saved by Jesus Christ, to the praise of God's grace in him and to the voiding of all boasting in himself? This he will surely deny. Is it a distrust of the truth of the gospel record?

This he dare not own. Is it a doubt of Christ's ability or goodwill to save? This is to contradict the testimony of God in the gospel. Is it because he doubts of an interest in Christ and his redemption? Tell him that believing on Christ makes up the interest in him. If he says that he cannot believe on Jesus Christ, because of the difficulty of putting this faith into practice, and that a divine power is needful to draw it forth which he does not have, tell him that believing in Jesus Christ is no work, but a resting on Jesus Christ; and that this pretence is as unreasonable as if a man wearied with a journey and unable to go one step further should argue, 'I am so tired that I am not able to lie down', when indeed he can neither stand nor go.

The poor wearied sinner can never believe on Jesus Christ till he finds he can do nothing for himself and in his first believing he always applies to Christ for salvation as a man hopeless and helpless in himself. And by such reasonings with him from the gospel the Lord will (as he has often done) convey faith and joy and peace by believing.

3. *This doctrine of free justification by faith alone has this advantage, that it suits all men's spirits and frames in their serious approaches to God in worship.*

Men may think and talk boldly of inherent righteousness and of its worth and value, of good works, and frames, and dispositions; but when men present themselves before the Lord, and have any discoveries of his glory, all things in themselves will disappear and be looked upon as nothing. Zophar, though the hottest speaker of Job's friends, did yet speak rightly to him (*Job* 11:4–5): 'For thou hast said, My doctrine is pure and I am clean in thine eyes. But oh, that God would speak!' And so Job found it, when God displayed his glory to him, and that only in the works of creation and providence (chapters 38, 39). He then changed his note (*Job* 40:4–5; 42:2–6). So it was with Isaiah (*Isa.* 6:5), till pardoning grace was imparted to him. No man can stand before this holy Lord God with any peace and comfort unless he have God himself to stay upon. His grace and mercy in Jesus Christ alone can preserve a man from being consumed; and the faith of it from being confounded. Hence we see the difference between men's minds in their disputes and doctrine about these points and their own sense and pleadings with God in prayer.

4. *This doctrine of justification by faith without any mixtures of man (by whatever names and titles they may be dignified or distinguished) has this undoubted advantage, that it is that to which all not judicially hardened and blinded do, or would, or must, betake themselves when dying.*

How reluctant men would be to plead that cause on a deathbed which they so stoutly stand up for with tongue and pen when at ease, and that evil day far away! They seem to be jealous lest God's grace and Christ's righteousness have too much room, and men's works too little, in the business of justification. But was there ever a sensible dying person exercised with this jealousy as to himself? Even bloody Stephen Gardiner,[1] when

---

[1] Bishop of Winchester, 1531–55, under Henry VIII and Mary Tudor, and a cruel persecutor of Protestants.

dying, could answer Dr Day, Bishop of Chichester, who offered comfort to him by this doctrine, 'What, my Lord, will you open that gap now? Then farewell altogether. To me, and such other in my case, you may speak it; but open this window to the people, then farewell altogether' (*Book of Martyrs*, vol. 3, p. 450). In which words he betrayed a conviction of the fitness of the doctrine to dying persons, and his knowledge that it tended to the destruction of the kingdom of Antichrist. So Foxe, in the same *Book of Martyrs*, vol. 2, p. 46, gives this as the reason of Luther's success against Popery, above all former attempts of preceding witnesses:

> But Luther gave the stroke, and plucked down the foundation, and all by opening one vein, long hid before, wherein lieth the touchstone of all truth and doctrine, as the only principal origin of our salvation, which is, our free justification, by faith only, in Christ the Son of God.

Consider how it is with the most holy and eminent saints when dying. Did you ever see or hear any boasting of their works and performances? They may and do own, to the praise of his grace, what they have been made to be, what they have been helped to do or suffer for Christ's sake. But when they draw near to the awful tribunal, what else is in their eye and heart but only free grace, ransoming blood, and a well-ordered covenant in Christ the Surety? They cannot bear to hear any make mention to them of their holiness, their own grace and attainments. In a word, the doctrine of conditions, qualifications and rectoral government, and the distribution of rewards and punishments according to the new law of grace, will make but an uneasy bed to a dying man's conscience; and will leave him in a very bad condition at present, and in dread of worse, when he is feeling, in his last agonies, that the wages of sin is death, if he cannot by faith add, 'But the gift of God is eternal life, through Jesus Christ our Lord' (*Rom.* 6:23).

He is a wise and happy man that anchors his soul on that rock at which he can ride out the storm of death. Why should men contend for that in their life that they know they must renounce at their death? Or neglect that truth now that they must betake themselves to then? Why should a man build a house which he must leave in a storm, or be buried in its ruins? Many architects have attempted to make a sure house of their own righteousness, but it is without a foundation and must fall, or be thrown down sorrowfully by the foolish builder, which is the better way. It is a great test of the truth of the doctrine about the way of salvation, when it is generally approved of by sensible dying men. And what the universal sense of all such in this case is, as to the righteousness of Christ and their own, is obvious to any man. He was an ingenious Balaamite who, being himself a Papist, said to a Protestant, 'Our religion is best to live in, and yours best to die in.'

5

Disadvantages of the True Doctrine of Justification

But notwithstanding these great advantages (and they are but a few of many) that this doctrine is attended with, there are not a few disadvantages it labours under; which, though they are rather to its commendation than its reproach, hinder its welcome and reception.

1. *This doctrine is a spiritual mystery, and does not lie level with a natural understanding (1 Cor. 2:10, 14).*

Working for life a man naturally understands, but believing for life, he understands not. To mend the old man, he knows; but to put on the new man by faith is a riddle to him. The study of holiness, and endeavouring to square his life according to God's law, he knows a little of, though he can never do it; but to draw sanctification from Christ by faith, and to walk holily in and through the force of the Spirit of Christ in the heart by faith is mere empty language to him.

A new life he understands a little; but nothing of a new birth and regeneration. He never saw himself stark dead. Nay, not only is it unknown to the natural man, but he is by his natural state an enemy to it. He neither does nor can know it, nor approve of it (*1 Cor.* 2:14). Wisdom (that is, Christ's way of saving men revealed in the gospel) is justified of all her children, and of them only (*Matt.* 11:19. *Luke* 7:29, 30, 35). This enmity in men to the wisdom of God is not only the cause of this contempt of its ministry, but is a temptation to many ministers to patch up and frame a gospel that is more suited to, and appealing to, and more easily understood by such men, than the true gospel of Christ is. This Paul complains of in others, and vindicates himself from (*1 Cor.* 1:17, and 2:2). He warns others against it (*Col.* 2:8; *2 Cor.* 11:3, 4; *Gal.* 1:6–9). And it is certain that *doing* for life is more suited to corrupt nature than *believing* is.

2. *Our opposers in this doctrine have the majority for them and against us as they of old boasted (*John* 7:48).*

This they have no ground to glory in, though they do; nor we to be ashamed of the truth, because we cannot compete in numbers with them. With our opposers are all these sorts (and they make a great number, though I do not say or think that all our opposers are to be ranked in any of these lists, for some, both godly and learned, may mistake us, and the truth, in this matter):

i. *They have all the ignorant people that know nothing of either law or gospel.* They serve God (they say, but most falsely); and hope that God will be merciful to them and save them. To all such, both the clear explication of God's law and the mysteries of the gospel are strange things. Yet sincere obedience they love to hear of, for all of them think there is some sincerity in their hearts, and that they can do something. But of faith in Christ they have no knowledge, unless by faith you understand a dream of being saved by Jesus Christ, though they know nothing of him, or of his way of saving men, nor of the way of being saved by him.

ii. *All formalists are on their side:* people that place their religion in trifles because they are strangers to the substance thereof.

iii. *All proud secure sinners are against us,* that go about, with the Jews, to establish their own righteousness (*Rom.* 10:3). The secure are whole, and see no need of the physician; the proud have medicine at home and despise that which came down from heaven.

iv. *All the zealous devout people in a natural religion are utter enemies to the gospel.* By a natural religion I mean that which is the product of the remnants of God's image in fallen man, a little improved by the light of God's Word. All such cannot endure to hear that God's law must be perfectly fulfilled in every tittle of it, or that no man can be saved by doing; that they must all perish for ever, that have not the righteousness of a man that never sinned, who is also God over all, blessed for ever, to shelter and cover them from a holy God's anger, and to render them accepted by him; that this righteousness is put on by the grace of God, and that a man must betake himself to it and receive it as a naked, blushing sinner; that no man can do anything that is good till gospel grace renews him and makes him first a good man.

This they will never receive, but still think that a man may grow good by doing good.

3. *Natural reason is very fertile in its objections and cavils against the doctrine of the grace of God, and especially when this corrupt reason is polished by learning and strong natural abilities.*

When there are many to broach such doctrine, and many so disposed to receive it, is it any wonder that the gospel truth makes little progress in the world? Nay, were it not for the divine power that supports it and the promises of its preservation, its enemies are so many and strong, and true friends so few and feeble, we might fear its perishing from the earth.

But we know it is impossible. And if the Lord has a design of mercy to these nations, and has a vein of his election to dig up amongst us, we make no doubt but the glory of Christ, as a crucified Saviour, shall yet be displayed in the midst of us, to the joy of all that love his salvation, and to the shame of others (*Isa.* 66:5).

4. *I might add: the great declension of some of the Reformed churches from the purity and simplicity of that doctrine they were first planted in.*

The New-Methodists[1] about the grace of God had too great an increase in the French churches. And, which was very strange, this declension advanced amongst them, at the same time when Jansenism[2] was spreading amongst many of the church of Rome, so that a man might have seen Papists growing better in their doctrine and Protestants growing worse. See Mr Gale's *Idea of Jansenism*, with Dr Owen's Preface. For what there is of this amongst us in England, I refer the reader to Mr Jenkyn's *Celeusma*, and to *The Naked Truth*, Part 4. And if there be any warping towards Arminian doctrine by some on our side, in order to ingratiate themselves with that church which has the secular advantages to dispense and to make way for some accommodation with them, I had rather wait in fear till a further discovery of it than offer to guess at it.

5. *Lastly, this doctrine lies under no small disadvantage from the spirit of the day we live in.*

A light, frothy, trifling temper prevails generally; doctrines of the greatest weight are talked of and

---

[1] Proponents of Amyraldianism, a view associated with Moïse Amyraut, a Protestant theology professor at Saumur, who taught that grace is universal in God's provision for salvation, but particular in its application to the elect alone.

[2] A movement within 17th and 18th Century Roman Catholicism, especially in France, which stressed God's efficacious grace in salvation. Though its proponents sought to reform Roman Catholicism from within, it was ultimately condemned by the papal bull *Unigenitus* in 1713.

treated about with a vain, unconcerned frame of spirit, as if men contended rather about opinions and school-points than about the oracles of God and matters of faith. But if men's hearts were seen by themselves, if sin were felt, if men's consciences were enlivened, if God's holy law were known in its exactness and severity, and the glory and majesty of the Lawgiver shining before men's eyes, if men were living as if leaving time and launching forth into eternity, the gospel salvation by Jesus Christ would be more regarded.

Objection 1: Is there not a great decay amongst professors in real practical godliness ? Are we like the old Protestants or the old Puritans ?

Answer: The decay and degeneracy is great, and heavily to be bewailed. But what is the cause and what will be its cure? Is it because the doctrine of morality and virtue and good works is not enough preached? This cannot be, for there has been for many years a public ministry in the nation that make these their constant themes. Yet the land is become as Sodom for all lewdness, and the tree of profaneness is so grown that the sword of the magistrate has not yet been able to lop off any of its branches. Is it because men have too much faith in Christ, or too little? Or none at all? Would not faith in Christ increase holiness? Did it not always do so? And will it not still do it? Was not the holiness of the first Protestants eminent and shining? And yet they generally put assurance in the definition of their faith. We cannot say that gospel-holiness has prospered much by the correction or mitigation of that seemingly harsh definition. The certain spring of this prevailing wickedness in the land is people's ignorance and unbelief of the gospel of Christ, and that grows through many prophets who speak lies to them in the name of the Lord.

Objection 2: But do not some abuse the grace of the gospel, and turn it into wantonness?

Answer: Yes, some do, ever did, and still will do so. But it is only the ill-understood and not believed doctrine of grace that they abuse. The grace itself, no man can abuse, for its power prevents its abuse. Let us see how Paul, that blessed herald of this grace (as he was an eminent instance of it) deals with this objection (*Rom.* 6:1, etc.). How does he prevent this abuse? Is it by extenuating what he had said (*Rom.* 5:20), that grace abounded much more where sin had abounded? Is it by mincing grace smaller so that men may not choke upon it or have too much of it? Is it by mixing something of the law with it, to make it more wholesome? No, but only by plainly asserting the power and influence of this grace, wherever it really is, as he does at length in that chapter.

This grace is all treasured up in Christ Jesus, offered to all men in the gospel, poured forth by our Lord in the working of faith, and drunk in by the elect in the exercise of faith. And it becomes in them a living spring, which will, and must, break out and spring up in all holy conversation. He exhorts them to drink in more and more of this grace by faith. And as for such as pretend to grace and live ungodly, the Spirit of God declares that they are void of grace, which is always fruitful in good works (*2 Peter* 2 and *Jude*).

The apostle orders the churches to cast such out (*1 Cor.* 5:2; *2 Tim.* 3:5); and to declare to them, as Peter did to a professor (*Acts* 8:20–21), that they have no part nor portion in this matter, for their heart is not right in the sight of God, though the doctrine is right that they hypocritically profess.

6

The Charge of Antinomianism Misapplied

But if our brethren will not forbear their charge of Antinomianism, we entreat them that they will make it justly, such as:

1. *Against those who say that the sanction of the holy law of God is repealed so that no man is now under it, either to be condemned for breaking it, or to be saved by keeping it,* which to us is rank Antinomianism and Arminianism both. Indeed, they say that the law does not now require perfect holiness. But what else can it require? For it is no law if its sanction is repealed.

2. *On those let the charge lie that are ungodly under the name of Christianity.* And both they and we know where to find such true Antinomians in great abundance, who

nevertheless are never called by that name. And is it not somewhat strange that men who have so much zeal against an Antinomian principle have so much kindness for true Antinomians in practice?

3. *Let him be called by this ugly name who does not judge the holy law and Word of God written in the Old and New Testament to be a perfect rule of life to all believers,* and does not admit that all should study conformity to this rule (*Rom.* 12:2).

4. *Against him who encourages himself in sin and hardens himself in impenitence by the doctrine of the gospel.* No man that knows and believes the gospel can do so. What some hypocrites may do is nothing to us, who disown all such persons and practices and own no principle that can really encourage the one or influence the other.

5. *Against him who thinks holiness is not necessary to all that would be saved.* We maintain not only that it is necessary to, but that it is a great part of, salvation.

6. *Against whoever thinks that when a believer comes short in obeying God's law he does not sin,* and that he ought not to mourn because of it as provoking to God and hurtful to the new creation in him, and that he need not renew the exercise of faith and repentance for repeated washing and pardoning.

7. *Against those who say that a sinner is actually justified before he is united to Christ by faith.* It is strange that such

as are charged with this, of all men do most press on sinners to believe on Jesus Christ and urge the damnation threatened in the gospel upon all unbelievers. That there is a decreed justification from eternity, particular and fixed as to all the elect, and a virtual, perfect justification of all the redeemed, in and by the death and resurrection of Jesus Christ (*Isa.* 53:11; *Rom.* 4:25; *Heb.* 9:26, 28 and 10:14) is not yet called in question by any amongst us; and more is not craved, but we affirm that a sinner, for his actual justification, must lay hold on and plead this redemption in Christ's blood by faith.[1]

But, on the other hand, we glory in any name of reproach (as the honourable reproach of Christ) that is cast upon us for asserting the absolute boundless freedom of the grace of God, which excludes all merit and everything like it; and the absoluteness of the covenant of grace – for the covenant of redemption was plainly and strictly a conditional one, and the noblest of all conditions was in it, the Son of God's taking on him man's nature and offering it in sacrifice being the strict condition of all the glory and reward promised to Christ and his seed (*Isa.* 53:10, 11) – wherein all things are freely promised, and that faith that is required for sealing a man's interest in the covenant is promised in it, and wrought by the grace of it (*Eph.* 2:8).

That faith at first is wrought by, and acts upon, a full and absolute offer of Christ, and of all his fulness – an offer that has no condition in it but that one native to all offers, acceptance; and in the very act of this

---

[1] This corrects William Twisse's error (see footnote on pp. 23–4), as does the Westminster Confession (XI:iv).

acceptance, the accepter expressly disclaims all things in himself but sinfulness and misery. That faith in Jesus Christ justifies (although, by the way, it is to be noted that it is never written in the Word that faith justifies actively, but it is always expressed passively: that a man is justified by faith, and that God justifies men by and through faith; yet admitting the phrase) only as a mere instrument, receiving that imputed righteousness of Christ, for which we are justified. And this faith, in the office of justification, is neither condition, nor qualification, nor our gospel-righteousness, but is in its very act a renouncing of all such pretences.

We proclaim the market of grace to be free (*Isa.* 55:1–3). It is Christ's last offer, and his lowest (*Rev.* 22:17). If there is any price or money spoken of, it is *no price, no money.* And where such are the terms and conditions, if we are forced to call them so, we must say that they look more like a renouncing than a boasting of any qualifications or conditions. Surely the terms of the gospel bargain are God's free giving and our free taking and receiving.

We are not ashamed of teaching:

The ineffectualness of the law, and all the works of it, to give life; either that of justification, or of regeneration and sanctification, or of eternal life;

That the law of God can only damn all sinners; that it only rebukes, and thereby irritates and increases sin; and that it can never subdue sin, till gospel grace comes with power upon the heart; and then when the law is written in the heart it is copied out in the life;

That we call men to believe on the Lord Jesus Christ, in that condition the first Adam brought them to and left them in; in that condition that the law finds and leaves them in, guilty, filthy, condemned; out of which condition they can only be delivered by Christ, and by believing on him;

That we tell sinners that Jesus Christ will surely welcome all that come to him; and, as he will not cast them out for their sinfulness, in their nature and past life, so neither will he do so for their misery, in the want of such qualifications and graces as he alone can give;

That we hold forth the propitiation in Christ's blood, as the only thing to be in the eye of a man that would believe on Christ unto justification of life; and that by this faith alone a sinner is justified, and God is justified in doing so;

That God justifies the ungodly (*Rom.* 4:5), neither by making him godly before he justifies him, nor by leaving him ungodly after he has justified him; but that the same grace that justifies him does immediately sanctify him;

If for such doctrine we are called Antinomians we are bold to say that there is some ignorance of, or prejudice against, the known Protestant doctrine in the hearts of the reproachers.

There are some things we complain of, such as:

1. *That they load their brethren so grievously with unjust calumnies, either directly or by consequence:* as when they preach up holiness, and the necessity of it, as if it were

their proper doctrine and disowned by us; when they cannot but know in their consciences that there is no difference between them and us about the nature and necessity of holiness, but only about its spring and place in salvation. We derive it from Jesus Christ and faith in him; and know assuredly that it can spring from nothing else. We place it between justification and glory, and that is its Scripture place; and no where else can it be found or stand, let them try it as much and as long as they will.

2. *That they seem very zealous against Antinomianism, and forget the other extreme of Arminianism;* which is far more common, as dangerous, and far more natural to all men. For though there have been, and may be this day, some true Antinomians, either through ignorance or weakness reeling to that extreme, or by the heat of contention with and hatred of Arminianism (as it is certain some very good and learned men have inclined to Arminianism through their hatred of Antinomianism, and have declared as much); and some may and do corrupt the doctrine of the gospel through the unrenewedness of their hearts; yet how destructive soever this abuse may be to the souls of the seduced, such an appearance of Antinomianism is but a meteor or comet that will soon blaze out and its folly will be quickly hissed off the stage. But the principles of Arminianism are the natural dictates of a carnal mind which is emnity both to the law of God and to the gospel of Christ; and, next to the dead sea of Popery – into which this stream also runs – they have, from Pelagius

to this day, been the greatest plague of the church of Christ and, it is likely, will be till his second coming.

3. *We also justly complain that, in their opposing of true Antinomian errors, and particularly the alleged tenets of Dr Crisp, they hint that there is a party of ministers and professors that defend them;* whereas we can defy them to name one minister, in London at least, that does so.

4. *That expressions capable of a good sense are strenuously perverted, contrary to the scope of the writer or speaker.* But this and methods like it are the usual methods of unfair contenders. Were the like methods taken on the other side, how many Popish, Arminian, yes, and Socinian expressions, might be published? If any gospel truth should be preached or published that reflects on the idol of self-righteousness, and justification thereby, it is soon quarrelled with. But reproaches cast on the free grace of God and the imputed righteousness of Christ are, with them, if not approved, yet but venial, well-meant mistakes. Let men's stated principles be known, and their expressions explained accordingly, or mistakes and contentions will be endless.

5. *We also complain that love to peace has made many grave and sound divines forbear to utter their minds freely in public on these points;* whereby the adverse party is emboldened; and such ministers as dare not purchase peace by silence, when so great truths are undermined, are exposed as a mark. But we do not question but that these worthy brethren, when they shall see the points of

controversy accurately stated (as they may shortly), will openly appear on truth's side, as we know their hearts are for it.

6. *Lastly, we complain that the scheme of the gospel contended for by our opposers is clouded, veiled, and darkened by school*[1] *terms;* new, uncouth, and unscriptural phrases, whereby, as they think to guard themselves against opposition, so they increase the jealousies of their brethren and keep their principles from the knowledge of ordinary people, who are as much concerned in those points as any scholar or divine.

This controversy looks like a very bad omen. We thought we might have healed our old breaches in smaller things; and, behold, a new one is threatened in the greatest matters. We did hope that the good old Protestant doctrine had been rooted and rivetted in the hearts of all the ministers on our side; but now we find the contrary, and that the sour leaven of Arminianism works strongly.

Their advocates do not yet own the name; but the younger sort are more bold and free. And with them no books or authors are in esteem and use but such as are for the new, rational method of divinity. *Rational* is a fitter commendation of a philosopher than of a divine; and yet it is somewhat better applied to a divine than to divinity; for true divinity has a higher and nobler origin than man's reason, even divine revelation; and it can never be rightly learned by those that do not have a

[1] i.e., scholastic

higher principle in them than reason, namely the teaching of the Holy Ghost. But as for Luther, Calvin, Zanchius,[1] Twisse, Ames, Perkins and divines of their spirit and stamp, they are generally neglected and despised.

We were in hope, that after the Lord had so signally appeared for his truth and people in preserving both under the rage of that Antichristian spirit of persecution and apostasy to gross Popery that wrought so mightily under the two last reigns, and when he had given us the long-desired mercy of a legal establishment of our gospel-liberty in this, that all hearts and hands should have been unanimously employed in the advancing of the work of Christ. But we find that, as we have for a long time lost, in a great measure, the *power*, we are now in no small danger of losing also the *purity* of the gospel. And without them, what does liberty signify!

There is no doubt that the devil designs to obstruct the course of the gospel. And in this he has often had the service of the tongues and pens of good men as well as of bad. Yet we are not without hope that the Lord, in his wisdom and mercy, will defeat him; and that these contentions may yet have good fruit and a good issue.

---

[1] Girolamo Zanchi (1516–90), a Reformed scholastic theologian who was a convert from Roman Catholicism.

7

'The Good Old Way of the Protestant Doctrine'

So that good may come out of this controversy, let me request a few things of my brethren.

1. *Let us not receive reports suddenly of one another.*
In times of contention, many false reports are raised and rashly believed. This is both the fruit and the fuel of contention. For all the noise of Antinomianism, I must declare that I do not know (and I have both opportunity and inclination to inquire) any one Antinomian minister or Christian in London who is really such as their reproachers paint them out, or such as Luther and Calvin wrote against.

2. *Let us make Christ crucified our great study, as Christians; and the preaching of him our main work, as ministers* (*1 Cor.* 2:2).

Paul determined to know nothing else. But many manage the ministry as if they had taken up a contrary determination, even to know anything save Jesus Christ and him crucified.

We are amazed to see so many ashamed of the cross of Christ, and to behave as if they accounted the tidings of salvation by the slain Son of God an old antiquated story, and unfit to be daily preached. And what comes in the place thereof is not unknown, nor is it worth the mentioning. For all things that come in Christ's place and jostle him out, either of hearts or pulpits, are alike abominable to a Christian.

How many sermons may a man hear, and read when printed, yea, and how many books are written about the way to heaven, wherein is hardly the name of Jesus Christ? And if he *is* named, it is the name of Christ as a Judge and Lawgiver, rather than as a Saviour. And as little room has Christ in many men's prayers; except it be in the conclusion.

When we cannot avoid the observing of those sad things, let it be a sharp spur to us to preach Christ more, to pray more in his name, and to live more to his praise. Let us not be deceived with that pretence that Christ may be preached when he is not named. The preaching of the gospel is the naming of Christ, and so explained (*Rom.* 15:20). And Paul was to bear Christ's name before the Gentiles, and kings, and the children of Israel (*Acts* 9:15).

3. *Let us study hard and pray much to know the truth and to cleave to it.*

It is an old observation, *Ante Pelagium securius loquebantur patres*, Before Pelagius even the fathers spoke more carelessly; meaning well and fearing no mistakes in their hearers. Now it is not so. We should be the more careful in our doctrine. Let us search our own consciences and see how we ourselves are justified before God. So Paul argued (*Gal.* 2:15, 16). And let us bring forth that doctrine to our people that we find in our Bibles and have felt the power of upon our own hearts.

4. *Let us not run into extremes, upon the right or left hand, through the heat of contention.*

Let us carefully keep the good old way of the Protestant doctrine wherein so many thousands of saints and martyrs of Jesus have lived holily and died happily, who never heard of our new schemes and notions.

And, for this end, let us take and cleave to the test of the Westminster Assembly's *Confession of Faith* and *Catechisms.* More we do not profess ourselves; more we do not crave of our brethren. And because we deal fairly and openly, I shall set down *verbatim* Chapter 11 of the *Confession*, Of Justification.

Article 1: Those whom God effectually calleth, he also freely justifieth: not by infusing righteousness into them, but by pardoning their sins, and by accounting and accepting their persons as righteous; not for any thing wrought in them, or done by them, but for Christ's sake

alone; not by imputing faith itself, the act of believing, or
any other evangelical obedience, to them, as their righteousness; but by imputing the obedience and satisfaction
of Christ unto them, they receiving and resting on him
and his righteousness by faith, which faith they have, not
of themselves, it is the gift of God.

Article 2: Faith, thus receiving and resting on Christ and
his righteousness, is the alone instrument of justification.
Yet it is not alone in the person justified, but is ever
accompanied with all other saving graces; and is no dead
faith, but worketh by love.

Article 3: Christ, by his obedience and death, did fully
discharge the debt of all those that are thus justified, and
did make a proper, real, and full satisfaction to his
Father's justice in their behalf. Yet, in as much as he was
given by the Father for them, and his obedience and
satisfaction accepted in their stead, and both freely, not
for any thing in them, their justification is only of free
grace; that both the exact justice, and rich grace of God,
might be glorified in the justification of sinners.

Article 4: God did, from all eternity, decree to justify all
the elect; and Christ did, in the fulness of time, die for
their sins, and rise again for their justification: nevertheless they are not justified, until the Holy Spirit doth, in
due time, actually apply Christ unto them.

Article 5: God doth continue to forgive the sins of those
that are justified; and although they can never fall from

the state of justification, yet they may, by their sins, fall under God's fatherly displeasure, and not have the light of his countenance restored unto them, until they humble themselves, confess their sins, beg pardon, and renew their faith and repentance.

Article 6: The justification of believers under the Old Testament was, in all these respects, one and the same with the justification of believers under the New Testament.

This is the whole chapter exactly.

Larger Catechism, Question 71:

How doth faith justify a sinner in the sight of God?

Answer: Faith justifies a sinner in the sight of God, not because of those other graces which do always accompany it; or of good works, that are the fruits of it; nor as if the grace of faith, or any act thereof, were imputed to him for his justification; but only as it is an instrument by which he receiveth and applieth Christ and his righteousness.

Let these weighty words be but heartily assented to in their plain and native sense and we are one in this great point of justification. But can any considering man think that the new scheme of a real change, repentance and sincere obedience as necessary to be found in a person that may lawfully come to Christ for justification; of faith's justifying as it is the spring of sincere obedience; of a man's being justified by, and upon his coming up to the terms of the new law of grace (a new word, but of an old and ill meaning); can any man think, that this scheme and the sound words of the Reverend Assembly do agree? Surely, if such a scheme had been offered to that grave, learned, and orthodox synod, it would have had a more severe censure passed upon it than I am willing to name.

Do we not find, in our particular dealings with souls, the same principles I am now opposing?

When we deal with the carnal, secure, careless sinners (and they are a vast multitude), and ask them a reason of that hope of heaven they pretend to, is not this their common answer?

I live inoffensively; I keep God's law as well as I can; and wherein I fail I repent and beg God's mercy for Christ's sake. My heart is sincere, though my knowledge and attainments be short of others.

If we go on to inquire further:

What acquaintance they have with Jesus Christ?
What applications their souls have made to him?
What workings of faith on him they have known?
What use they have made of his righteousness for
   justification and his Spirit for sanctification?
What they know of living by faith in Jesus Christ?

we are barbarians to them. And in this sad state many thousands in England live and die and perish eternally. Yet so thick is the darkness of the age that many of them live here and go hence with the reputation of good Christians; and some of them may have their funeral sermon and praises preached by an ignorant flattering minister; though it may be the poor creatures never did, in the whole course of their life, nor at their death, employ Jesus Christ so much for an entry to heaven purchased by his blood and only accessible by faith in him, as a poor Turk does Mahomet for a place in his beastly paradise. How common and fearful a thing is this in this land and city!

When we come to deal with a poor awakened sinner, who sees his lost state, and that he is condemned by the law of God, we find the same principles working in him, for they are natural and therefore universal in all men and hardly rooted out of any.

We find him sick and wounded. We tell him where his help lies, in Jesus Christ; what his proper work is, to apply to him by faith. What is his answer? 'Alas!', says the man, 'I have been and I am so vile a sinner, my heart is so bad and so full of plagues and corruptions, that I cannot think of believing on Christ. But if I had but repentance, and some holiness in heart and life, and such and such gracious qualifications, I would then believe', when indeed this answer is as full of nonsense, ignorance, and pride, as words can contain or express. They imply:

1. If I were pretty well recovered, I would employ the Physician, Christ.
2. That there is some hope to work out these good things by myself, without Christ.
3. And when I come to Christ with a price in my hand I shall be welcome.
4. That I can come to Christ when I will.

So ignorant are people naturally of faith in Jesus Christ; and no words or warnings repeated, nor the plainest instructions, can beat into men's heads and hearts, that the first coming to Christ by faith, or believing on him, is not a believing we shall be saved by him; but a believing on him, that we may be saved by him. And it is less to be wondered at, that ignorant people do not, when so many learned men will not, understand it.

When we deal with a proud, self-righteous hypocrite we find the same principles of enmity against the grace of the gospel. A profane person is not so enraged at the rebukes of sin from the law as these Pharisees are at the discovery of their ruin by unbelief. They cannot endure to have their idol of self- righteousness touched, either by the spirituality of God's law, that condemns all men and all their works while out of Christ; or by the gospel, which reveals another righteousness than their own, by which they must be saved; but they will have God's ark of the covenant to stand as a captive in the temple of their Dagon of self-righteousness, until the vengeance of God's despised covenant overthrow both the temple, and idol, and worshippers.

There is not a minister that deals seriously with the souls of men but he finds an Arminian scheme of justification in every unrenewed heart. And is it not sadly to be bewailed, that divines should plead that same cause that we daily find the devil pleading in the hearts of all natural men? And that instead of *casting down* (*2 Cor.* 10:4–5) they should be *making defences for* such strong holds as must either be levelled with the dust or the rebel that holds out in them must eternally perish?

It is no bad way of studying the gospel, and of attaining more light in it, to deal particularly with the consciences of all sorts of men, as we have occasion. More may be learned this way than out of many large books. And if ministers would deal more with their own consciences and the consciences of others in and about these points that are most properly cases of conscience, we should find an increase of gospel light, and a growing fitness to preach aright, as Paul did: 'By manifestation of the truth commending ourselves to every man's conscience in the sight of God' (*2 Cor.* 4:2).

Let us keep up, in our hearts and doctrine, a reverent regard of the holy law of God and not suffer a reproachful, disparaging word or thought of it. The great salvation is contrived with a regard to it; and the satisfaction given to the law by the obedience and death of Christ our surety has made it glorious and honourable, more than all the holiness of saints on earth or of the glorified in heaven, and more than all the torments of the damned in hell, though they do also magnify the law, and make it honourable.

But if men will teach that the law and obedience to it, whether perfect or sincere, is the righteousness we must be found in and stand in, in our pleading for justification, they neither understand what they say nor whereof they affirm (*1 Tim.* 1:7). They become debtors to the law, and Christ profits them nothing (*Gal.* 2:21 and 5:2, 5).

And we know what will become of that man that has his debts to the law to pay, and has no interest in the surety's payment. Yet many such offer their own silver which, whatever coin of man is upon it, is reprobate and rejected both by law and gospel.

Let us carefully keep the boundaries between the law and the gospel clear, which 'whosoever doth, is a right perfect divine', says blessed Luther, in his *Commentary on the Epistle to the Galatians,* a book that has more plain sound gospel than many volumes of some other divines. Let us keep the law as far from the business of justification as we would keep condemnation, its contrary. For the law and condemnation are inseparable, except by the intervention of Jesus Christ our Surety (*Gal.* 3:10–14). But in the practice of holiness, the fulfilled law given by Jesus Christ to believers as a rule is of great and good use to them, as has been declared.

Lastly, be exact in your communion and church administrations. If any walk otherwise than becomes the gospel, if any abuse the doctrine of grace to licentiousness, draw the rod of discipline against them the more severely, since you know so many are watching for your failures, and are ready to speak evil of the ways and truths of God.

The wisdom of God sometimes orders the different opinions of men about his truth for the clearing and confirming of it; while each side watch the extremes that others may be in hazard of running into. And if controversy is fairly and meekly managed in this way we may differ and plead our opinions and both love and edify those we oppose and be loved and edified by them in their opposition,

I know no fear possessing our side but that of Arminianism. Let us be fairly secured from that and, as we ever hated true Antinomianism, so we are ready to oppose it with all our might. But having such grounds of jealousy as I have named – and it is well known that I have not named all – men will allow us to fear that this noise of Antinomianism is raised, and any advantage our opponents have through the rashness and imprudence of some ignorant men is inflated to a severe height by some on purpose, in order to shelter Arminianism in its growth and to advance it further amongst us; which we pray and hope the Lord will prevent.

8

Postscript: The Vital Importance of the Doctrine of Justification

The discourse now presented was originally intended as a private letter to a particular brother, as the title shows. How it came to be published, I shall not trouble the world with an account of.

I think that Dr Owen's excellent book on *Justification*[1] and Mr Marshall's book on the *Gospel Mystery of Sanctification*[2], by faith in Jesus Christ, are such vindications and

[1] *The Doctrine of Justification by Faith through the Imputation of the Righteousness of Christ Explained, Confirmed and Vindicated* (1677), *Works of John Owen*, vol. 5 (reprinted London: Banner of Truth, 1965).

[2] See p. 14.

confirmations of the Protestant doctrine as to admit of no effectual opposition. Dr Owen's name is so savoury and famous, his soundness in the faith and ability in learning for its defence so justly reputed, that no sober man will attempt to refute him.

Mr Marshall was a holy retired person and is only known to most of us by his book published lately. The book is a deep, practical, well-jointed discourse and requires a more than ordinary attention to read it with profit. And if it is honestly used I look upon it as one of the most useful books the world has seen for many years.

Its excellency is that it leads the serious reader directly to Jesus Christ and cuts the sinews and over-turns the foundation of the new divinity by the same argument of gospel-holiness by which many attempt to overturn the old. And as it already has the seal of high approbation by many judicious ministers and Christians that have read it, so I have no fear but that it will stand firm as a rock against all opposition and will prove good seed, and food, and light and life, to many hereafter.

All my design in publishing this is, plainly and briefly, to give some information to ordinary plain people who lack either time or judgment to peruse large and learned tractates about this point of justifica-tion, wherein every one is equally concerned.

The theme of justification has suffered greatly by this, that many have employed their heads and pens who never had their hearts and consciences exercised about it. And they must be frigid and dreaming speculations that all such are taken up with whose consciences are not enlivened with their personal concern in it. These things are undoubted:

1. *That as it is a point of highest concern to every man, so it is to the whole doctrine of Christianity.* All the great fundamentals of Christian truth centre in this of justification. The Trinity of Persons in the Godhead; the incarnation of the only begotten of the Father; the satisfaction paid to the law and justice of God for the sins of the world by his obedience and sacrifice of himself in that flesh he assumed; and the divine authority of the Scriptures which reveal all this: these are all straight lines of truth that centre in this doctrine of the justification of a sinner by the imputation and application of that satisfaction.

There can be no justification without a righteousness; no righteousness can suffice but that which answers fully and perfectly the holy law of God; no such righteousness can be performed but by a divine person; no benefit can accrue to a sinner by it unless it is in some way his and applied to him; no application can be made of this but by faith in Jesus Christ. And as the connection with and dependence of this truth upon the other great mysteries of divine truth is evident in the plain proposal of it, so the same has been sadly manifest in this, that the forsaking of the doctrine of justification by faith in Christ's righteousness has been the first step of apostasy in many who have not stopped till they revolted from Christianity itself.

Hence so many Arminians, and their chief leaders too, turned Socinians. From denying justification by

Christ's righteousness, they proceeded to the denying of his satisfaction; from the denial of his proper satisfaction, they went on to the denying of the divinity of his person. And that man's charity is excessive that will allow to such blasphemers of the Son of God the name of Christians. Let not then zeal for so fundamental a point of truth as that of the justification of a sinner by faith in Christ be charged with folly. 'It is good to be zealously affected always in a good thing' (*Gal.* 4:18), and this is the best of things.

2. *It is undoubted that there is a mystery in this matter of justification.* As it is God's act, it is an act of free grace and deep wisdom. Herein justice and mercy kiss one another in saving the sinner. Here appears the God-man, with the righteousness of God, and this is applied and imputed to sinful men. Here man's sin and misery are the field in which the riches of God's grace in Christ are displayed. Here the sinner is made righteous by the righteousness of another, and obtains justification through this righteousness, though he pays and gives nothing for it. God declares him righteous, or justifies him freely; and yet he is well paid for it by the redemption that is in Christ Jesus (*Rom.* 3:24–26). It is an act of both justice and mercy when God justifies a believer on Jesus Christ. And must there not then be a great mystery in it? Is not every believer daily admiring the depth of this way of God?

This mystery is usually rather darkened than illustrated by logical terms used in the handling of it. The only defence that good and learned men have for the use of them (and it has great weight) is that the craft of adversaries constrains them to use such terms, to expose or hedge in the opposers. It is certain that this mystery is as plainly revealed in the Word as the Holy Ghost thought fit to do in teaching the heirs of this grace; and it would be well if men did contain themselves within these bounds.

3. *It is certain that this doctrine of justification proposed in the Word has been very differently understood and expressed,* by men that profess that God's Word is the only rule of their thoughts and words about the things of the Spirit of God. It has been, and will be still, a stone of stumbling, as our Lord Jesus Christ himself was and is (*Rom. 9:32–33; 1 Pet. 2:7–8*).

4. *It is also true that whatever variety and differences there are in men's notions and opinions (and there are a great many) about justification, they are all certainly reducible to two;* one of which is every man's opinion. And they are that the justification of a sinner before God is either

on the account of a righteousness in and of ourselves; or

on the account of a righteousness in another, even Jesus Christ, who is Jehovah our righteousness.

Law and gospel, faith and works, Christ's righteousness and our own, grace and debt, do equally divide all in this matter. Crafty men may endeavour to blend and mix these things together in justification, but it is a vain attempt. It is not only most expressly rejected in the gospel, which peremptorily determines the contrariety, inconsistency and incompatibility between these two; but the nature of the things in themselves, and the sense and conscience of every serious person, witness to the same thing, that our own righteousness and Christ's righteousness comprehend all possible pleas of men to justification – one or other of them every man in the world stands upon – and that they are inconsistent with, and destructive of, one another in justification.

If a man trusts to his own righteousness, he rejects Christ's; if he trusts to Christ's righteousness, he rejects his own. If he will not reject his own righteousness, as too good to be renounced, if he will not venture on Christ's righteousness, as not sufficient alone to bear him out and bring him safely off at God's bar, he is in both convicted as an unbeliever. And if he endeavours to patch up a righteousness before God made up of both, he is still under the law, and a despiser of gospel grace (*Gal.* 2:21). That righteousness that justifies a sinner consists in *aliquo indivisibili*, something indivisible; and this every man finds when the case is his own, and he serious about it.

5. *These different sentiments about justification have been at all times managed with a special acrimony.* Those that are for the righteousness of God by faith in Jesus Christ look upon it as the only foundation of all their hopes for eternity, and therefore they cannot but be zealous for it. And the contrary side are as hot for their own righteousness, the most admired and adored Diana of proud mankind, as if it were an image fallen down from

Jupiter (see *Acts* 19:21–41); when it is indeed the idol that was cast out of heaven with the devil, and which he has ever since been so diligent to set up before sinful men to be worshipped, so that he might bring them into the same condemnation with himself. For by true sin, and false righteousness, he has deceived the whole world (*Rev.* 12:9).

6. *As the Holy Ghost speaking in the Scriptures is the supreme and infallible judge and determiner of all truth, so where he does particularly and on purpose deliver any truth, there we are specially to attend and learn.* And though, in most points of truth, he usually teaches us by a bare authoritative narration, yet in some points, which his infinite wisdom foresaw special opposition to, he not only declares but debates and determines the truth.

And the instances are two especially. One is about *the divinity of Christ's person, and the dignity of his priesthood,* reasoned, argued, and determined in the epistle to the Hebrews. The other is about *justification by faith,* exactly handled in the epistles to the Romans and to the Galatians. In the former of these two the doctrine of free justification is taught us most formally and accurately.

And though we find no charge against that church, in Paul's time, or in his epistle, for their departing from the truth in this point, yet the wisdom of the Holy Ghost is remarkable in this, that this doctrine should be so plainly asserted, and strongly proved, in an epistle to that church the pretended successors of which have apostatized from that faith, and become the main assertors of that damnable error of justification by works.

The epistle to the Galatians is plainly written to cure a begun and obviate a full apostasy from the purity of the gospel in the point of justification by faith without the works of the law.

And from these two epistles, if we are wise, we must learn the truth of this doctrine and expound all other Scriptures in a harmony with what is there so deliberately determined, as *in foro contradictorio* (in a court of appeal).

7. *Lastly it is not to be denied or concealed that on each side some have run into extremes, which the generality do not own but are usually loaded with.* The Papists run high for justification by works, yet even some of them, in the Council of Trent, discoursed very favourably of justification by faith. The Arminians have qualified a little the grossness of the Popish doctrine in this article, and some since have essayed to qualify that of the Arminians, and to plead the same cause more finely.

Again, some have run into the other extreme, as appeared in Germany a little after the Reformation; and some such there have been always, and in all places where the gospel has shed its light; and these were called *Antinomians*. But how unjustly this hateful name is charged upon the orthodox preachers and sincere believers of the Protestant doctrine of justification by faith only, who keep the gospel middle-way between these two rocks, it is the purpose of this discourse to demonstrate. What we plead for is, in sum:

i. that Jesus Christ our Saviour is the fountain opened in the house of David for sin and for uncleanness

(*Zech.* 13:1), wherein alone men can be washed in justification and sanctification; and

ii. that there is no other fountain of man's devising, nor of God's declaring, for washing a sinner first, so as to make him fit and qualified to come to this, to wash and to be clean.

As for inherent holiness, is it not sufficiently secured by the Spirit of Christ received by faith, the certain spring and cause of it; by the Word of God, the plain and perfect rule of it; by the declared necessity of it to all those who look to be saved, and to justify the sincerity of a man's faith; unless we bring it into justification, and thereby make our own pitiful holiness sit on the throne of judgment, with the precious blood of the Lamb of God?

Though I expect that a more able hand will undertake an examination of the new divinity, yet, to fill up a little room, I would speak somewhat to their Achillean argument that is so much boasted of and so frequently insisted on by them as their shield and spear. Their argument is this: that Christ's righteousness is our *legal* righteousness; but our own is our *evangelical* righteousness: that is, When a sinner is charged with sin against the holy law of God, he may oppose Christ's righteousness as his legal defence; but against the charge of the gospel, especially for unbelief, he must produce his faith, as his defence or righteousness, against that charge.

With a great deference to such worthy divines as have looked on this as an argument of weight, I shall, in a few words, attempt to manifest that this is either a repetition, in other odd words, of what is commonly taught by us; or a deceptive fallacy; or a departure from the Protestant doctrine about justification.

1. *This argument does not at all concern the justification of a sinner before God.*

For this end, no more is needful than to consider what this charge is, against whom it is given, and by whom. The charge is said to be given in by God; and it is a charge of unbelief, or disobeying the gospel. But against whom? Is it against a believer or an unbeliever? And these two divide all mankind. If it is against a believer, it is a false charge and can never be given in by the God of truth. For the believer is justified already by faith and as to this charge he is innocent. And innocence is defence enough to a man falsely charged, before a righteous judge. Is this charge given in against an unbeliever? We allow it is a righteous charge.

'Aye, but,' say they, 'will Christ's righteousness justify a man from this charge of gospel-unbelief?' The answer is plain. No, it will not; nor yet from any other charge whatsoever, either from law or gospel; for he has nothing to do with Christ's righteousness while an unbeliever. What then does this arguing reprove (*Job* 6:25)? Is it that no man's faith in Christ's righteousness can be justified in its sincerity before men and in a man's own conscience but in and by the fruits of a true lively faith? In this they have no opposers that I know of. Or is it that a man may have Christ's righteousness for his legal righteousness, and yet be a rebel to the gospel, and a stranger to true holiness? Who ever affirmed it? Or is it that this gospel-holiness is that which a man must not only have – for that we grant – but also may venture to stand in, and to be found in before God, and to venture into judgment with God upon, in his claim to eternal life? Then we must oppose them that think so, as we know their own consciences will when in any lively exercise.

These plain principles of gospel-truth, while they remain – and remain they will on their own foundation, when we are all in our graves and our foolish contentions are buried – do overthrow this pretended charge.

i. That Christ's righteousness is the only plea and answer of a sinner arraigned at God's bar for life and death.

ii. That this righteousness is imputed to no man but a believer.

iii. That when it is imputed by grace, and applied by faith, it immediately and eternally becomes the man's righteousness, before God, angels, men, and devils (*Rom.* 8:33, 35, 38, 39). It is a righteousness that is never lost, never taken away, never ineffectual, answers all charges, and is attended with all graces.

2. *I would ask, What is that righteousness that justifies a man from the sin of unbelief?*

We have rejected the imaginary charge; let us now consider the real sin. Unbelief is the greatest sin against both law and gospel; more remotely against the law, which binds all men to believe God speaking, say what he will; more directly against the gospel, which tells us what we should believe, and commands us to believe.

Let us put this case (and it is pity the case is so rare, when the sin is so common), that a poor soul is troubled about the greatness of the sin of unbelief, in calling God a liar (*1 John* 5:10), in distrusting his faithful promise, in doubting Christ's ability and good will to save, in standing aloof so long from Jesus Christ; as many of the elect are long in a state of unbelief till called, and the best of believers have unbelief in some measure in them (*Mark* 9:24). Abraham's faith staggered sometimes (*Gen.* 12 and 20). What shall we say to a conscience thus troubled? Will any man dare to tell him that Christ's righteousness is his legal righteousness against the charge of sins against the law, but for gospel-charges, he must answer them in his own name? I know our hottest opposers would abhor such an answer, and would freely tell such a man that the blood of Jesus Christ cleanses from all sin and that his justification from his unbelief must be only in that righteousness which he so sinfully had rejected while in unbelief and now lays hold on by faith.

3. *But some extend this argument yet more dangerously; for they say:*

Not only must men have their faith for their righteousness against the charge of unbelief, but repentance against the charge of impenitence, sincerity against that of hypocrisy, holiness against that of unholiness, and perseverance as their gospel righteousness, against the charge of apostasy.

If they mean only that these things are justifications and fruits of true faith and of the sincerity of the grace of God in us, we agree to the meaning but highly dislike the expressions, as unscriptural and dangerous, tending to the dishonouring of the righteousness of Christ, and to run men on the rocks of pride and self-righteousness, that natural corruption drives all men upon. But if they mean, that, either jointly or separately, they are our righteousness before God; or that, either separate from or mixed with Christ's righteousness, they may be made our claim and plea for salvation; I must say that it is dangerous doctrine and that its native tendency is to turn Christ's imputed righteousness out of the church, to destroy all the solid peace of believers, and to exclude gospel-justification out of this world and reserve it to another, and that with a horrible uncertainty of any particular man's partaking of it.

But these blessed truths of God and blessings of believers stand on firmer foundations than heaven or earth and will continue fixed against all the attempts of the gates of hell. Blessed be the rock, Christ, on which all is built; blessed be the new covenant, ordered in all things and sure; and blessed is he that believeth, for there shall be a performance of those things which are told him from the Lord (*Luke* 1:45). Amen.

SOME OTHER
BANNER OF TRUTH
TITLES

THE DOCTRINE OF JUSTIFICATION BY FAITH,

THROUGH THE IMPUTATION OF THE RIGHTEOUSNESS OF CHRIST, EXPLAINED, CONFIRMED AND VINDICATED

John Owen

Owen's masterly account of justification by faith, first printed in 1677, is distinguished from other classic works on the subject by a dominating pastoral concern. The core of his work is straightforward biblical exposition, massive, fresh, compelling and practical.

'I have had no other design', wrote Owen, 'but only to enquire diligently into the divine revelation of the way . . . whereby the conscience of a distressed sinner may attain assured peace with God through our Lord Jesus Christ.'

The book has been blessed in just such a way to many from Owen's time till now.

Volume 5 of the
Works of John Owen

ISBN 0 85151 067 1
457 pp. Cloth-bound

THE DOCTRINE OF JUSTIFICATION

AN OUTLINE OF ITS HISTORY
IN THE CHURCH AND OF ITS
EXPOSITION FROM SCRIPTURE

James Buchanan

'This robust classic of James Buchanan on the doctrine of justification is biblical, solid and refreshing . . . We heartily commend this book and thank the Banner of Truth Trust for its reappearance in such an attractive format, in large clear print.'

FREE PRESBYTERIAN MAGAZINE

'Every minister should have this work, and every serious-minded Christian should be encouraged to read it.'

EVANGELICAL MOVEMENT OF WALES

'If Luther was right that justification is the article of a standing or falling church, it is time that this work was read again, for we know of nothing in English on the same scale since his day.'

EXPOSITORY TIMES

ISBN 0 85151 440 5
534 pp. Cloth-bound

The PURITAN PAPERBACKS series:

All Loves Excelling, John Bunyan
ISBN 0 85151 739 0, 139 pp.
All Things for Good, Thomas Watson
ISBN 0 85151 478 2, 128 pp.
Apostasy from the Gospel, John Owen
ISBN 0 85151 609 2, 184 pp.
The Art of Prophesying, William Perkins
ISBN 0 85151 689 0, 206 pp.
The Bruised Reed, Richard Sibbes
ISBN 0 85151 740 4, 138 pp.
The Christian's Great Interest, William Guthrie
ISBN 0 85151 354 9, 208 pp.
Communion with God, John Owen
ISBN 0 85151 607 6, 224 pp.
The Doctrine of Repentance, Thomas Watson
ISBN 0 85151 521 5, 128 pp.
Glorious Freedom, Richard Sibbes
ISBN 0 85151 791 9, 208 pp
The Glory of Christ, John Owen
ISBN 0 85151 661 0, 184 pp.
The Godly Man's Picture, Thomas Watson
ISBN 0 85151 595 9, 256 pp.
A Puritan Golden Treasury, I. D. E. Thomas,
ISBN 0 85151 249 6, 320 pp.
Heaven on Earth, Thomas Brooks
ISBN 0 85151 356 5, 320 pp.
The Holy Spirit, John Owen
ISBN 0 85151 698 X, 216 pp.
Learning in Christ's School, Ralph Venning
ISBN 0 85151 764 1, 297 pp.

Letters of Samuel Rutherford
ISBN 0 85151 163 5, 208 pp.
A Lifting Up for the Downcast, William Bridge
ISBN 0 85151 298 4, 288 pp.
The Mystery of Providence, John Flavel
ISBN 0 85151 104 X, 224 pp.
Prayer, John Bunyan
ISBN 0 85151 090 6, 176 pp.
Precious Remedies Against Satan's Devices,
Thomas Brooks,
ISBN 0 85151 002 7, 256 pp.
The Rare Jewel of Christian Contentment,
Jeremiah Burroughs
ISBN 0 85151 091 4, 232 pp.
The Reformed Pastor, Richard Baxter
ISBN 0 85151 191 0, 256 pp.
The Shorter Catechism Explained from Scripture,
Thomas Vincent
ISBN 0 85151 314 X, 280 pp.
The Sinfulness of Sin, Ralph Venning
ISBN 0 85151 647 5, 284 pp.
A Sure Guide to Heaven, Joseph Alleine
ISBN 0 85151 081 7, 148 pp.
The True Bounds of Christian Freedom,
Samuel Bolton
ISBN 0 85151 083 3, 224 pp.

For free illustrated catalogue please write to
THE BANNER OF TRUTH TRUST

3 Murrayfield Road,   P O Box 621, Carlisle,
Edinburgh EH12 6EL   Philadelphia 17013,
UK   USA